A WISH YOU WERE HERE® BOOK

YOSEMITE

THE CYCLE OF THE SEASONS

LYNN WILSON ◆ JIM WILSON ◆ JEFF NICHOLAS

ISBN O-939365-29-4 (Revised Edition Paperback)
O-939365-30-8 (Revised Edition Clothbound)

Printed in Singapore.
First Edition: 1990, (ISBN 0-939365-13-8[Pb], -17-0[Cl])
Second Edition: 1991
Third Edition: 1993 (Revised)
Fourth Edition: 1995

SIERRA PRESS, INC.

4988 Gold Leaf Drive, Mariposa, CA 95338

CONTENTS

DEDICATION

*This book is dedicated
to those who stop;*

to see, to hear, to smell, to taste, to feel,

*not just to know,
but to understand.*

ACKNOWLEDGEMENTS

We would like to take this opportunity to express our gratitude to Len McKenzie, former Chief Park Naturalist, for his years of tireless effort on behalf of Yosemite National Park and for his dedication to passing on to the visitor all that we know and understand about Yosemite as a living environment. It is because of the selfless dedication by individuals such as Len that the National Parks, despite shrinking budgets and massive increases in visitation, continue to be the inspiring places they are for most visitors.

INTRODUCTION
by Jeff Nicholas

There are few places on earth which so stir the soul as Yosemite National Park. Whether seen from the summit of a 13,000-foot peak in the backcountry or viewed through the sun-dappled shade of a riverside cottonwood in Yosemite Valley, this is a land of superlatives. Half Dome, Tuolumne Meadows, El Capitan, these landmarks are as well known in Europe and Asia as they are in America.

Since its 'discovery' in 1851, Yosemite's beauty has attracted painters, writers and photographers. Thomas Moran and Alfred Bierstadt were so overwhelmed they were led to gross overstatement. John Muir spent much of his life attempting to capture in words some fleeting semblance of this landscape. Fiske, Watkins and Muybridge brought back vivid evidence of this landscape's wonders, triggering the tide of visitors who would follow to see, experience and discover for themselves, this glorious work of Nature.

Today's visitors, be they artists or seekers of beauty, owe a great debt to these first adventurers. Without their dedication and perseverance our national parks might not exist today. Considered by many to be the 'crown jewels' of the American landscape, our national parks are much more than landmarks and infinitely more than mere curiosities. They are, rather, refuges of the human spirit; landscapes against which one can measure one's self. We are reminded of our own insignificance and at the same time of our oneness with all life.

It was not so long ago in the history of mankind, that 'wild' places were the norm, not the exception. It is not surprising that great energy was expended in taming these 'wild' places, in converting them to our use, transforming them to our needs. The nineteenth century poet, Walt Whitman, wrote:

"...Nature is rude and incomprehensible at first; be not discouraged, keep on, there are divine things well envelop'd, I swear to you there are divine things more beautiful than words can tell."

Today, this 'rude, incomprehensible' Nature is cherished. We travel great distances and exert great energy to see what is left of these 'wild' places. Many consider these places sacred, more important for what they are than for any use mankind might make of them.

Today's first-time visitor to Yosemite will most assuredly be overwhelmed by the grandeur of the landscape. Towering monoliths and thundering waterfalls are irresistible sirens vying for our attention. One's attention may also be drawn to the more 'mundane'; the texture of granite, the pattern of pine needles strewn on the forest floor, the sighing of an afternoon breeze as it passes through meadow grasses, "divine things more beautiful than words can tell".

We hope, as publishers of this volume, to intimately share Yosemite

EL CAPITAN, AUTUMN SUNSET.

with the reader. We have chosen images of both the grand and the subtle. We also hope this book will act as a catalyst to memory and as an insight into one's self. We ask that you share these beauties and insights with your friends, your neighbors, and especially your children so that they too might better understand the importance of our continued vigilance and hard work to preserve such "rude, and incomprehensible" places.

ABOUT THE REVISED EDITION

It is with great pride that we bring this revised edition of "Yosemite: The Cycle of the Seasons" to the marketplace. Not only have we added dozens of new images, many by nationally renowned artists, we have also added an essay on the environment of the Park and its surroundings. In addition we have provided a park map and expanded information on the plant communities of Yosemite.

We hope these additions will enhance the reader's, or the visitor's, understanding and appreciation of this complex organism we call Yosemite.

Finally, those of you who may own the earlier edition of this title will notice dramatic improvements in the quality of design and reproduction. These changes have been made in order to provide the reader with a truer reproduction of the artist's vision

So now, sit back, turn the page, and enjoy...
                              ...Yosemite, the Cycle of the Seasons.

YOSEMITE: A Living Landscape

By Jim Wilson

In 1864, President Abraham Lincoln concluded that America's great scenic resources were neither unlimited nor indestructible. He summoned the courage to do what no previous individual had ever done: to set aside a piece of wilderness—Yosemite Valley and the Mariposa Grove of giant sequoias— "for public use, resort and recreation" with the intention that they "shall be inalienable for all time." It was the birth of a bold new concept, the withdrawal of land from private ownership to be used for public use and preservation. Through many decades his wisdom has proven invaluable, for America now has the finest system of national parks and recreation areas in the world.

The setting aside of these parcels proved to be only the first step in the evolution of our modern-day concept of conservation and preservation. In 1868 John Muir, a young man who had emigrated to America from Scotland, was drawn to the "Range of Light." Seeking adventure, he hired on as a shepherd in Yosemite's high country. In addition to his job-related duties, he found time to study the effect men and their imported livestock had on this newly discovered pristine and fragile landscape. These observations eventually led to his intensive endeavors to protect and preserve more of his beloved wilderness. John Muir had an unusual affection for these high meadows and their wild inhabitants. This love led him to a passionate study of the ongoing natural processes of the Sierra Nevada. Through eloquent writing and intense lobbying efforts, John Muir, as well as numerous additional conservationists, pressed for expanded preservation of much of the Sierra Nevada. Meanwhile, President Lincoln's concept of preserving public lands for the purpose of "resort and recreation" gained widespread acceptance and, in 1878, Congress created America's first "national park," Yellowstone. In September of 1890 Sequoia became our second national park and one week later nearly 2 million acres surrounding the land grant tracts of Yosemite Valley and Mariposa Grove were preserved as Yosemite National Park (today's Park boundaries include only 760,000 acres).

Most first-time visitors to Yosemite are attracted by stories of its stunning landscape. These visitors come to view, for themselves, the sublime spectacles of sheer cliffs, spectacular waterfalls, and massive domes of granite. They may inadvertently find themselves asking, for the first time: How were these extraordinary natural features formed? and Why are they here? when confronted by such a foreign landscape. In Yosemite, climate and geology have come together in a very dramatic fashion to create whole communities of plants and animals and a unique, unforgettable landscape. This book celebrates Yosemite's visual splendor and the flora and fauna that live in this special place.

BLACK OAKS, LATE AUTUMN/EARLY WINTER.

GEOGRAPHY

Yosemite National Park encompasses 1,189 square miles and preserves three major features: High Sierra wildlands, groves of giant sequoias, and Yosemite Valley. Elevations inside the Park's boundaries range from 2,000 feet in the western foothills to more than 13,000 feet on the eastern mountain crest. The Park is located in the central portion of the 400-mile-long Sierra Nevada, a young mountain range that forms an elevated spine extending nearly half the length of California. The unusual heights of the range, up to 14,500 feet in places, mean that it blocks the flow of winter storms arriving from the west. Weather in the Sierra is notoriously changeable, while to the east the Mojave Desert sits parched in an enormous rain shadow. The Sierra Nevada has a unique profile: its western side forms a long, gradual slope, while the eastern escarpment of the range is characterized by nearly vertical rises of up to 10,000 feet. Erosion has sculpted the land on the western side of the Sierra. Today the spectacular results of this erosion are preserved in Yosemite and Sequoia/Kings Canyon national parks.

GEOLOGY

The earth is approximately 4.6 billion years old, but the Sierra Nevada is relatively young in comparison. Most geologists believe the land mass that, as a result of continental drift and plate tectonics, underlies our West Coast arrived in this proximity about 250 million years ago. According to this theory, the westward drifting North American Continental Plate collided with the Pacific Plate. With nowhere for the plates to go but one over the other

(known as *subduction*), the Pacific Plate was thrust under the North American Plate. Molten magma rose to near the surface and cooled and solidified. It is generally thought that the Sierran batholith was formed between 130 and 85 million years ago. By about 20 million years ago continuing plate movement, magmatic activity, volcanism, and erosion had created a land of rolling hills, broad valleys, and meandering streams.

Then, about 10 million years ago, volcanic activity once again occurred, and finally the pre-glacial Sierra Nevada took shape. Its massive form extended more than 400 miles long and 80 miles wide, angling from northwest to southeast along a fault line extending through today's Owens Valley. As it continued to rise, this granitic terrain cracked along numerous fractures, which formed areas of contrasting strengths and weaknesses. As the mountains rose, slippage along eastside faults caused a large eastern segment to drop, forming the Owens Valley and leaving the steep escarpment that is evident today.

As time passed watercourses formed, which followed major granitic fractures westward across the gradual slope to the Great Central Valley. Two rivers formed in the Yosemite area: the Merced River carved Yosemite Valley, and the Tuolumne River sculpted the Grand Canyon of the Tuolumne and Hetch Hetchy. Between 10 and 3 million years ago, the climate grew cooler and drier, allowing great coniferous forests to become dominant. During this time span the land continued to rise and was subject to relentless erosion. The steeper gradient caused the Merced and Tuolumne rivers to cut down in their courses and form distinct v-shaped canyons, as deep as 3,000 feet. Side streams such as Bridalveil, Illilouette, and Yosemite creeks could not keep pace and subsequently became steep cascades tumbling into the main river.

GLACIATION

Ice Age glaciation is responsible for most of the striking rock forms in Yosemite today. Glaciers form when snow falls and accumulates at a rate greater than the annual melt. Under great pressure from overlying layers of snow and compressed crystals the ice becomes hard packed, eventually forming glacial ice. As a glacier gains in weight and mass, gravity begins to work. The ice slowly creeps downward, moving, in the Sierra, at a rate of up to one to two inches per day. Glaciers erode, then leave behind glacial deposits, which form many recognizable signs on the landscape, the most prominent of which are gouged and quarried valleys. It is unknown exactly how many periods of glaciation occurred in and around the Park, but many scientists believe that areas of the Sierra Nevada have been sculpted by moving ice for most of the past 3 million years. Yosemite itself may have been subject to perhaps 30 or more glacial advances. During a period of maximum glacia-

tion, around 750,000 years ago, this region was completely submerged beneath a sea of ice, except for the tallest of domes and peaks. In Yosemite Valley, Half Dome stood a mere 700 feet above the ice, Sentinel Dome barely peeked through, and El Capitan was completely covered. Yosemite's major glaciers formed on the cooler slopes of Mounts Lyell, Dana, and Conness, and even though many glaciers overflowed canyon rims and ridge crests, most of their carving force was focused deep in the river canyons.

In addition to quarried valleys, glaciers left behind other telltale signs. They were responsible, in large part, for the unique shape of many Sierran peaks. The names given these shapes are strange and often French, names such as *cirque, horn, arête, col,* and *roche moutonnée.* With some keen observation, today's visitors can locate prominent examples of these formations throughout Yosemite's high country. *Cirques* are bowl-shaped basins on the slopes of peaks and ridges, left behind as glaciers quarried the weaker, fractured granite and carried it down-canyon. *Horns* form when the headwalls of several cirques erode toward each other, leaving a sharp peak such as Unicorn Peak. An *arête* is a jagged ridge, and a *col* is a low pass—both occurring between two cirques. A *roche moutonnée* is an asymmetric dome over which a glacier once flowed. It is characterized by a gradual slope on the up-canyon side and, due to intense downward pressure, a steep, quarried angle on the leeside. Prominent examples, Lembert and Pothole domes, can be seen in Tuolumne Meadows.

Free-standing granite boulders deposited far from their origin, and known as *erratics,* are frequently seen in the high country, as is *glacial polish,* a smooth and shiny granitic surface. Several types of moraines may also be found, including *lateral moraines,* deposits of debris left along the margins of glacial flows, and *terminal moraines*, ridges of debris deposited at the farthest point of advancement prior to recession. Lakes typically form either behind a terminal moraine or in shallow depressions quarried from hard rock during a glacier's advance.

Ice floes often extended more than 60 miles down the Tuolumne River drainage, into the v-shaped Grand Canyon of the Tuolumne and Hetch Hetchy Valley. Concurrently, some of the Tuolumne River Valley ice crossed a ridge and flowed into the Merced River drainage, passing through both the Little Yosemite Valley and Tenaya Canyon and joining once again at the base of Half Dome. The ice quarried Yosemite's canyons into ever deeper troughs, leaving tributary streams such as Bridalveil Creek to leap a sheer wall, creating a formation known as a *hanging valley*. The final period of Yosemite Valley glaciation occurred 10,000 years ago during the last ice age. After that, the climate warmed and glaciers receded. This final glacier was incapable of further excavation or erosion and eventually died at a point near the base of El Capitan, leaving a terminal moraine that, when it filled with water, formed ancient Lake Yosemite. Silt gradually replaced water, leaving behind the relatively level floor of today's Yosemite Valley.

Common belief holds, and it is true throughout most of the world, that glacial-carved valleys are almost always u-shaped. The question arose repeatedly among many early geologists, why then are most all of Yosemite's canyons now v-shaped? There is absolutely no doubt that glaciers marched down the Grand Canyon of the Tuolumne and Tenaya Canyon yet they are unmistakably v-shaped. In fact Yosemite Valley appears to be the only "classic" u-shaped canyon in the Park. The answer to the v-shape riddle came when geologists learned that, as the molten rock of the Sierra Nevada cooled, it fractured, forming joints. These joints provided a path of least resistance which the glaciers moved down, plucking out the pre-fractured granite. The seemingly contradictory shape of Yosemite Valley was clarified when seismic tests revealed that sediments forming the valley floor are up to 2000 feet deep instead of the previously believed 300 feet. It turns out that, in fact, Yosemite Valley is v-shaped. The exaggerated depth and shape of the Valley are the result of the unique size, spacing, and alignment of the joints in this area.

SHAPING CONTINUES

The story of Yosemite's formation did not end with periods of glaciation. This landscape is very young and remains dynamic and ever changing, although it seems slow by human standards. An occasional earthquake still takes its toll, as do wind, rain, winter frost, and snow avalanches. All of these forces have helped erode Yosemite's walls, leaving behind talus slopes at the base of nearly every major landmark. Vegetation also contributes to the continuing sculpture. Tree and shrub roots grow into cracks causing them to widen, then water seeps into the ever-widening crevices and freezes during cold weather. In time granite weakens, gravity takes its toll, and tons of rock crash to the valley below, oftentimes claiming the tree or trees in the process.

The role of water in shaping and forming Yosemite's distinctive landscape is unmistakable. The evidence can be seen throughout the Park, in the many v-shaped canyons and hanging valleys created by massive ice floes. Water is also the main ingredient in Yosemite's most popular visitor attractions: waterfalls. The most obvious of the Park's waterfalls are in Yosemite Valley where Yosemite Falls and Bridalveil Fall are on display. Even in late summer, during the driest of years, water can be seen leaping over the precipices of the Giant's Staircase (Vernal, Nevada, and Illilouette falls), however, the best time for viewing waterfalls is in late spring or early summer.

At 2,425 feet, the three sections of Yosemite Falls attract, by far, the most attention. The 1,430-foot Upper Fall is connected to the 320-foot Lower Fall by the 675-foot Middle Cascade. During peak runoff, the noise of crashing and thundering water rattles windows in nearby buildings. However, the first waterfall most visitors see upon entering Yosemite Valley is 620-foot Bridalveil Fall. When viewed in spring, from Tunnel View observation point on Highway 41, it is obvious how this stunning waterfall obtained its name. From Glacier Point, two other major falls may be seen descending the Giant's Staircase: 594-foot Nevada Fall and 317-foot Vernal Fall. These waterfalls make a pleasant destination for a day hike that begins at Happy Isles, in the eastern end of Yosemite Valley. Approximately halfway up the Vernal Fall trail is an excellent view of a third waterfall in this area of the Park: Illilouette Fall. In spite of its relative obscurity, more water will plunge over Illilouette each year than over Yosemite Falls. In addition to the major waterfalls, springtime visitors to Yosemite will be able to see many seasonal waterfalls, including Sentinel, Ribbon, Royal Arch Cascade, Horsetail, Lehamite, Staircase, and Silver Strand falls.

Waterfalls are not restricted, however, to Yosemite Valley. They can be found in almost every region of the Park. In the Wawona area, a short hike will lead to the cascades of Chilnualna Falls, the total height of which ranks it among the Park's highest waterfalls outside Yosemite Valley. There are three major waterfalls in the Hetch Hetchy area: Wapama, Tueeulala, and Rancheria falls. Along Highway 140, on the western edge of the Park, are Cascade and Wildcat falls and, in a relatively short hike from Tuolumne Meadows, one can see an impressive succession of falls, including Tuolumne, White Cascade, California, LeConte, and Waterwheel falls.

The mountains themselves are, in large part, responsible for wringing moisture from the heavens. Water-laden clouds sweep in from the Pacific Ocean and quickly encounter a tall barrier: the Sierra Nevada. As the clouds are forced upward, temperatures drop, and moisture grows, which is released in the form of rain and snow. This seasonal deluge of water not only fuels the Park's waterfalls but is responsible for its rich biotic diversity.

In few other locations can such a variety of life zones be explored. Yosemite's biotic wealth of birds, mammals, shrubs, trees, and flowering plants is distributed vertically. In this steep topography and varied climate one can experience "spring" for six consecutive months. Spring's first blush begins in the Park's low elevations, around El Portal and the Merced River Canyon in early March. The season progressively unfolds through increasingly higher elevations, until it expires in the uppermost reaches of the alpine region by late summer. By beginning on the Park's western boundary and traveling to the summit of its highest peak, visitors ascend more than two vertical miles and pass through five scientifically classified life zones. In descending the more arid east side of the Sierra to Mono Lake 1.3 of those vertical miles are lost, giving rise to substantially different plant communities. In traveling those few miles west to east,

visitors experience the same plant communities that would otherwise require more than 2,000 miles of travel ranging from the Sonoran Desert of Northern Mexico to the Arctic Circle of northern Canada.

The system of grouping types of plants together and confining them to specific zones was first outlined by C. Hart Merriam during his travels in the Grand Canyon region in the 1800s. Since then, however, we have come to realize that Merriam's life zone system is fraught with exceptions. Nature will rarely allow itself to be grouped into neat and tidy categories; however, the "plant community" system, put in proper perspective, can be useful in understanding Yosemite's biotic diversity. A familiarity with certain plant groupings allows us to predict what types of birds and animals may inhabit an area. In the Merced River Canyon, the **Oak Woodland Zone** (Upper Sonoran) supports oak, redbud, manzanita, willow, and cottonwood. In this zone, the

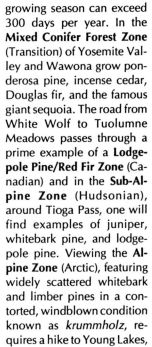

growing season can exceed 300 days per year. In the **Mixed Conifer Forest Zone** (Transition) of Yosemite Valley and Wawona grow ponderosa pine, incense cedar, Douglas fir, and the famous giant sequoia. The road from White Wolf to Tuolumne Meadows passes through a prime example of a **Lodgepole Pine/Red Fir Zone** (Canadian) and in the **Sub-Alpine Zone** (Hudsonian), around Tioga Pass, one will find examples of juniper, whitebark pine, and lodgepole pine. Viewing the **Alpine Zone** (Arctic), featuring widely scattered whitebark and limber pines in a contorted, windblown condition known as *krummholz*, requires a hike to Young Lakes, Mount Dana, or Mount Hoffman. So little research has been conducted in this Arctic-like tundra region that no one is absolutely certain how short the growing season really is. Two additional communities found on the eastern slope are the **Jeffrey Pine/Sagebrush Zone** (Upper Sonoran) containing pinyon and Jeffrey pines, aspen, and sagebrush. The second is the **Sagebrush Scrub Zone** (Lower Sonoran) featuring sagebrush, rabbitbrush, and mountain mahogany. (Local terminology for each life zone is listed first with the corresponding Merriam name·in parenthesis. Refer to the map and graphic beginning on page 96 for additional details).

TOPOGRAPHY

Lush west-slope forests, beneficiaries of greater precipitation, stand in stark contrast to the semi-arid eastern escarpment. Upon reaching Mono Lake the elevation is 6,400 feet, about the same as Lake Tahoe, yet it is surrounded by high desert of the Great Basin. Water is an essential ingredient in supporting life, and this mountain range, acting as an impediment, disproportionately allocates water wealth. Water, to a large degree, determines who and what can live where. Water and climate are but two factors that influence the distribution of Yosemite's life forms. In addition to climatic influences dictated by elevation, topographical features are responsible for the creation of microclimates. For example, Snow Flat receives approximately twice as much annual snowfall as does Tuolumne Meadows, even though they are about the same elevation. Snow Flat is situated to the

south of Mount Hoffman and consequently collects snow from approaching storms, while Tuolumne Meadows is in the "rain shadow" of the Cathedral Range. Another influencing factor of topography is the distribution of vegetation associated with the direction a slope faces. A north-facing slope receives less direct sunlight, experiences less evaporation, and consequently supports a denser and more diverse stand of vegetation.

With the addition of soil to the equation, the stage is set for life to prosper in the Sierra. Most soil found in Yosemite has been formed from a granite base. Decomposing and crumbling granite accumulates in flat locations and forms a deep, well-drained bed. Jeffrey pine, white fir, oak, and many shrubs grow well in this basic soil, but as time passes other processes create ingredients that contribute to soil enrichment. Rivers and streams transport silt, while vegetation dies and—with the aid of bacteria, fungi, and invertebrates—decomposes. Animals such as gophers, squirrels, moles, and badgers then take over and churn it all together. The end result is a rich humus that will support a remarkably diverse variety of insects, trees, plants, animals, and birds.

FIRE!

This interdependent system works so well that over a prolonged period of time the buildup of humus and forest litter can become so thick that it retards or prevents germination and growth of seedlings. Enter fire. Fire unlocks naturally occurring nutrients stored in organic material. In addition to creating ash, the thick humus is reduced and the forest floor is once again opened up. Nature's way of igniting vegetation is through lightning. Native Americans, such as the Miwok of the Yosemite area, seemed to understand the benefits of fire, for they would periodically burn grasslands as well as the forest floor. This would promote the growth of tuberous plants and encourage healthy and productive oak trees, both being important food sources.

There are some trees that have adapted to and depend on fire for their

GIANT SEQUOIAS IN MARIPOSA GROVE.

prosperity and survival. The giant sequoia, due to extremely slow growth, experiences difficulty competing for light with other faster-growing species. Well-timed fires will slow or eliminate competitive species. In addition, this mammoth denizen has bark that is extremely fire-resistant, while its seeds can only be released following fire. Seeds from other coniferous trees as well as shrubs and wildflowers also get a boost from fire. Ceonothus, a shrub favored as browse by mule deer, responds particularly well after a fire. With the lack of fire a habitat moves steadily toward a climax stage, that is a mature, single-species forest. A climax forest is not an environment that encourages diversity in either plants or wildlife, so, in the absence of fire, nature attempts other solutions. One such solution, visible along the Tioga Road, east of Tenaya Lake, was a needleminer moth infestation that left the climax forest of lodgepole pines nothing but a stand of ghost trees. The dead trunks are still visible today, but in their place grows a healthy and diverse woodland.

Fire seemed to have a natural place in the ecosystem until Europeans arrived on the Yosemite scene, some 150 years ago, and attempted to protect their wooden buildings by suppressing fires. From that arrival in Yosemite until 1971, and even later in the surrounding forest lands, every fire was doused as quickly as humanly possible. As Yosemite became more developed, its inhabitants became more proficient at putting out naturally occurring fires. The buildup of duff and litter helped to increase volatility and intensity when a fire did occur—a situation that led to the National Park Service, guardians of Yosemite

National Park, to find new solutions to the dilemma. A better understanding of fire now allows park personnel to develop new policies that permit natural fires to run their course. Small remedial or management fires are even deliberately set. Swift action, however, is still taken to extinguish, as quickly as possible, any fire—man-caused or natural—that threatens human life, property, or improvements. Science has learned that natural and periodic fires are an integral part of a healthy ecosystem and as such play a vital role in promoting life.

OUR HERITAGE

....after ten years spent in the heart of it, rejoicing and wondering, bathing in its glorious floods of light, seeing the sunbursts of morning among the icy peaks, the noonday radiance on the trees and rocks and snow, the flush of alpenglow and a thousand dashing waterfalls with their marvelous abundance of irised spray, it still seems to me above all others the Range of Light. —John Muir

Mr. Muir gazes and gazes, and cannot get his fill. —Joseph LeConte

It is now our right and privilege to be able to gaze upon and marvel at the same Yosemite that inspired John Muir. It is no longer necessary to get our fill today, for we are assured— Yosemite will be here tomorrow.

CYCLES
By Lynn Wilson

"This grand show is eternal.
It is always sunrise somewhere;
the dew is never all dried at once;
a shower is forever falling;
vapor is ever rising.
Eternal sunrise, eternal sunset,
eternal dawn and gloaming..."
John Muir

STAR TRAILS ABOVE SENTINEL DOME.

WINTER

HOWLING COYOTE, WINTER AFTERNOON.

I wish you were here, for Yosemite is an avenue of beauty and tranquility. From lush valley meadows, to thunderous waterfalls, from peace in the high country, to stunning granite massifs. All its splendors, great and small, captivate your entire being and allow your mind to drift into a zone of nonexistent time.

Listen- for today is the first day of Winter and it is hushed by the sound of nothing. Silently, soft, white puffs of heaven-sent manna quilt the earth. Snow flocked black oaks starkly contrast the pure white fluff resting on their dark branches. The air is clean and crisp, bearing the frigid fragrance of fresh frozen vapor.

Occasionally the silence is broken by frolicsome coyote pups, playfully yipping and crunching the crystaline meadows as they toss and roll about, or the whispering of deer as they browse through snow to find the cache of Autumn's stubble. And suddenly, during a rare moment, cloaked in the powder-blue fog of predawn, comes a chilling prehistoric croak of a great blue heron as it lifts from a frozen pond.

Against the lapis sky of Winter's midmorn, a muffled plopping sound echoes across the valley floor as sunstruck trees drop their snowy burden on the unsuspecting. Ruddy cheeks and icy moustaches uplift and are warmed by the hovering orb while backs stay chilled from its diminished rays.

Still, deep in sleepy shadows, are icy dreams of days gone by and glaciers yet unborn.

EL CAPITAN, WINTER MORNING.

HALF DOME, WINTER AFTERNOON.

MERCED RIVER AT THE BASE OF CATHEDRAL ROCK. 20

GIANT SEQUOIA AFTER WINTER STORM, MARIPOSA GROVE.

MERCED RIVER & SENTINEL ROCK, WINTER SUNSET.   22

HORSETAIL FALL, LATE WINTER AFTERNOON.

SNOWY PINES AT THE BASE OF EL CAPITAN   24

REFLECTIONS IN THE MERCED RIVER, EARLY MORNING.

THE 'ACORN' & BLACK OAKS IN EL CAPITAN MEADOW.

INCENSE CEDAR IN THE SNOW.

THE MERCED RIVER NEAR VALLEY VIEW, WINTER MORNING. 28

HALF DOME & EL CAPITAN, WINTER STORM.

WINTER SUNSET FROM VALLEY VIEW.

WINTER REFLECTIONS, MERCED RIVER.

FOXTAIL PINE WITH RIME ICE.

ICE CRYSTALS & REFLECTION OF HALF DOME.

SPRING

RED-WINGED BLACKBIRD & COW PARSNIP.

Listen- for today is the first day of Spring. Mating migrators offer day-break songs of love as they delicately prepare for the advent of new life. Gentle showers moisten faces as warm breezes dry them off. Trees rustle in the wind. Fruit blossoms intoxicate the air and rivers first taste the now liquid snow.

Lime-green leaves unfurl overnight and fecund meadows ooze with the thawing of Winter. There is a light scent of decay as nutrients prepare for the coming rebirth, even the earth-bound fog carries the musty odor. Snow laden peaks melt into thundering waterfalls plummeting fluid comets to the quaking earth. Treetop babes brazenly cry to be fed while discarded pinecones from hungry squirrels bounce limb to limb with a final thump on the needle carpeted floor.

Perfumed foothills trade snowflake for blossom and a distinct bouquet from flower painted roadsides welcomes in the season. Emerald meadows are hued with butterflied horizons while droning bees dance atop wild Iris. Yellow banners of heady scented tree pollen wave across the heavens while the fresh aroma of new grass and the smell of spearmint spices the Valley floor.

Water splashes in boulder strewn rivers, and twittering Ouzels dip into the rapids. Chirping crickets and croaking frogs line the raging shores to harmonize with the aquatic song, while high above, soaring on unseen thermals, birds of prey write silent lyrics across the sky.

In the still of night, the massive, jagged brow of Half Dome is graced with a myriad of brilliant stars. Warm moonlit walks reveal hidden faces in stone, yellow blossoms of Evening Primrose and drenching mists from forever high falls are crowned with a lunar rainbow.

NEVADA FALL & LIBERTY CAP, LATE AFTERNOON.

SHOWY MILKWEED IN YOSEMITE VALLEY.

HALF DOME AS VIEWED FROM THE DIVING BOARD, SUNSET.

DOGWOOD BRACTS AGAINST INCENSE CEDAR TRUNK.   40

CATHEDRAL ROCKS FOLLOWING A SPRING STORM.

SNOW PLANTS AT CRANE FLAT.

DOGWOODS ALONG AVALANCHE CREEK.

MAMMOTH PEAK & KUNA CREST, EARLY SPRING IN DANA MEADOW.   44

WILDCAT FALL, SPRING RUN-OFF.

GIANT SEQUOIAS IN THE MARIPOSA GROVE.

TUOLUMNE RIVER, SPRING RUN-OFF, SUNSET.

CASCADE CREEK IN SPRING FLOOD.

DOGWOOD ALONG THE MERCED RIVER.

MONKEYFLOWER & CORN LILY IN SUMMIT MEADOW.

BRIDALVEIL FALL AT SUNSET.

VERNAL FALL, LATE AFTERNOON.

SUMMER

WESTERN GRAY SQUIRREL EATING A PINE CONE.

Listen- for today is the first day of Summer. Thunder echoes between the grandiose walls. Lightning illuminates blackened sky with blinding flashes of energy and wisps of rain from a passing cloud tap glisten the granite to a wet silver-gray.

Strong, long and mighty, the sun no longer hides its warmth in shadow. Summer leaves, green with chlorophyll, gather strength to bear fruit. Tender babes of the earth begin to venture on their own. Youthful beldings peek from earthen holes. Fledgling grosbeaks frantically flap as they hit the ground with a graceless thunk. Spotted fawns play chase the butterfly and tiny trout make heroic leaps for the prized fly.

Misty rainbows and the balm of ozone provide refreshment on steep trails to lofty peaks. Here, high in the alpine, glorious bouquets decorate the barren slopes with splashes of intense color. Sun warmed rocks and an ancient breeze become ideal companions for an afternoon nap.

Yearning for peace, we find solitude in the alpine. A haven to draw within oneself, void of the ticking we gauge our lives by. The tranquility of the wilderness draws us into a relaxed state of mind. Everything a complement to everything else, we realize, we too, are a complement of nature.

Here we rest.
Here we gain.
The expanse.
The serenity.
The absolute quiet of the high country.

LeCONTE FALLS, GRAND CANYON OF THE TUOLUMNE RIVER.   56

BRACKEN FERN & INCENSE CEDAR CONE.

HALF DOME FROM OLMSTED POINT, SUNSET.

HALF DOME & FOG FROM WASHBURN POINT.

OTTOWAY LAKE & MERCED PEAK, LATE AFTERNOON. 60

GRASS, ROCK & POOL NEAR OLMSTED POINT.

MT. ANSEL ADAMS, LYELL FORK OF THE MERCED RIVER.   62

SUNSET FROM THE SUMMIT OF MT. HOFFMAN.

GIANT SEQUOIA TRUNKS IN MARIPOSA GROVE.

CATHEDRAL PEAK & LOWER CATHEDRAL LAKE BASIN.

VERNAL POOL IN TUOLUMNE MEADOWS, SUNSET.

PONDEROSA PINE SEEDLINGS IN EL CAPITAN MEADOW. 68

MULE DEER WITH VELVET ANTLERS.

GLACIAL POLISH NEAR OLMSTED POINT, SUNSET.   70

SHORE OF LAKE TENAYA, SUMMER.

WATERWHEEL FALL & RAINBOW, TUOLUMNE RIVER.   72

GLACIAL ERRATICS AT OLMSTED POINT, SUNSET.

AUTUMN

GREAT BLUE HERON & MERCED RIVER.

Listen- for today is the first day of Autumn. Squirrels begin preparing for Winter and a feverish pitch of gathering takes dominion over their day. Dried leaves rustle about as they bury even more acorns. With cheeks bulging, they scamper into the earth and ready their warm winter's nest. They fatten and add a thicker, more luxurious coat.

In the early light of dawn, beneath a blanket of wispy fog, the meadows sleep. Last night's campfire smoke still lingers in the air. Summer dissolves before our eyes and memories of Autumns past cloud the present.

There is a departure of green from the leaves as chlorophyll retreats. Hemp threads the meadows with gold, while Dogwoods, Maples, and Oaks add a bouquet of incredible brilliance and again the Valley becomes a kaleidoscope of colors.

Afternoon gusts sweep dried branches and showers of multi-hued leaves tinkle from above. Swirling winds corral the bristling displays and gently rest them on sleepy ground. At dusk, El Capitan sparkles with climbers' flashlights as they bid the slumbering Valley goodnight. Save for the repeated howl of coyotes baying at the moon, there is an absence of woodland sounds. Rings of fire fill the chill of twilight with a smokey aroma and campers huddle to glowing embers as the cool of night draws near.

Days shorten and even the mighty icons reach to the sun with a warm glow of gold. Waterfalls slow to a trickle and the river becomes a meandering current of multi-colored leaves.

SENTINEL ROCK, AUTUMN SUNSET.

SHORELINE OF SIESTA LAKE, AUTUMN.

INDIAN HEMP & GRASSES BY THE MERCED RIVER.

AUTUMN NEAR THE MERCED RIVER.

EL CAPITAN, EARLY AUTUMN MORNING.

DOGWOOD & MAPLE LEAVES IN FERN SPRING.

LICHEN ENCRUSTED GRANITE & MAPLE LEAF.

ASPENS IN BOHLER CANYON, MONO BASIN.

HALF DOME SEEN FROM STONEMAN MEADOW.

WILD GINGER & MAPLE LEAVES, AUTUMN.

TREES & FOG, WAWONA ROAD.

BLACK OAKS IN EL CAPITAN MEADOW.

STREAM & FALLEN LEAVES NEAR FERN SPRING.

EL CAPITAN & MERCED RIVER, AUTUMN SUNSET.

HALF DOME & MERCED RIVER, AUTUMN SUNSET.

WINTER

A BRIEF REPRISE

Listen—for today is the first day of Winter and it is hushed by the sound of nothing. I wish you were here, to share in the warm benedictions of these seasons. To be moved by Nature's rhythm, captured in her zone of non-existent time. And upon parting, allowing the "whole" of Yosemite's treasures, to become your mind's secret hiding place.

EL CAPITAN, MID-WINTER MORNING.

PHOTOGRAPHIC CREDITS

Fred Benz: Front Cover,7.
Carr Clifton: 32,44,56,68,72,88.
Charles Cramer: 18,49,87.
Chris Falkenstein: 22,23,69,70,92.
Michael Frye: 16,21,34,54,74.
Jeff Gnass: 5.
Jeff Grandy: 1,6,11,77.
William Neill: 10,48,63,84.
Jeff Nicholas: 8,12,13,14,19,25,28,31,43,45,51,53,59,
    61,66,67,71,73,79,82,89,94.
Jeff Nixon: 62.
Pat O'Hara: 9,37,60,86.
Jim Stimson: 83.
Tom Till: 39.
Larry Ulrich: 41,47,65,76,80,85,90.
Keith S. Walklet: 20,24,33,40.
Jim Wilson: 15,26,27,29,30,36,38,42,46,50,52,57,58,
    64,78,81,91.
Copyrights to all photographs are held by the artists.

CREDITS

"Cycles" by Lynn Wilson.
"Introduction" by Jeff Nicholas.
"Yosemite: A Living Landscape" by Jim Wilson.
Map of Yosemite by Jeff Nicholas.
"The Plant Communities of Yosemite" by Jeff Nicholas.
Book design by Jeff Nicholas.
Editor for this project: Nicky Leach.
Layout and design performed on a Macintosh Quadra 900
utilizing Aldus PageMaker and Microsoft Word. All texts set
in Palatino and Optima Typefaces on a Lasermaster 1000.
Printing coordinated by TWP, Ltd., Berkeley, Ca.

SUGGESTED READING

Bakker, Elna. *An Island Called California*. (1971) Reprint.
    Berkeley: University of California Press, 1972.
Brower, Kenneth. *Yosemite: An American Treasure*. Wash-
    ington, D.C.: National Geographic Society, 1990.
Johnston, Verna R. *Sierra Nevada*. Boston: Houghton Mifflin
    Co. 1970.
Lopez, Barry H. *River Notes: The Dance of Herons*. Kansas
    City; Andrews and McMeel, Inc.,1979.
Lopez, Barry H. *The Rediscovery of North America*. Lexing-
    ton: University of Kentucky Press, 1990.
Muir, John. *The Yosemite*. (1912). Reprint. Garden City:
    Doubleday and Company, 1962.
Orland, Ted. *Man & Yosemite: A Photographers View of the
    Early Years*. Santa Cruz: Image Continuum Press,
    1985.
Reid, Robert L. (Editor). *A Treasury of the Sierra Nevada*.
    Berkeley: Wilderness Press, 1983.
Schaffer, Jeffrey P. *Yosemite National Park*. (1978). Reprint.
    Berkeley: Wilderness Press, 1983.
Storer, Tracy & Usinger, Robert. *Sierra Nevada Natural His-
    tory*. Berkeley: University of California Press, 1963.
Wilson, Lynn & Wilson, Jim & Nicholas, Jeff. (1987). Reprint
    Wildflowers of Yosemite. Yosemite: Sierra Press,
    Inc.,1992.
The Yosemite Association, one of many non-profit organiza-
tions chartered by Congress to aid the National Parks, is an
excellent source of affordably priced guides, pamphlets and
books. Their publications may be found at the sales areas in
Visitor Centers or by contacting them directly:

The Yosemite Association
PO Box 230
El Portal, CA 95318
(209) 379-2646

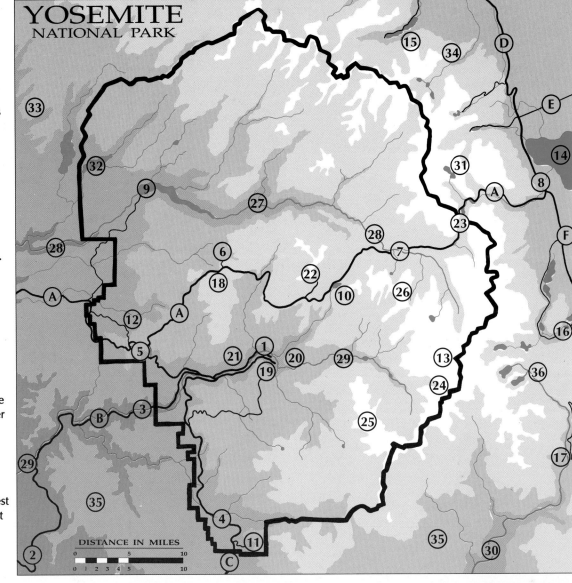

YOSEMITE
NATIONAL PARK

DISTANCE IN MILES

0   5   10

0 1 2 3 4 5   10

ALPINE (Arctic Zone)	SUB-ALPINE (Hudsonian Zone)	LODGEPOLE-RED FIR (Canadian Zone)	MIXED CONIFER (Transition Zone)	OAK WOODLAND (Upper Sonoran Zone)